P9-CAF-405

Between Towns

Between Towns

Poems by Laurie Kutchins

Texas Tech University Press

This book was set in 11 on 15 Galliard and printed on acid-free paper that meets the guidelines for permanence and durability of the Committee on Production Guidelines for Book Longevity of the Council on Library Resources. ♾

Printed in the United States of America

Library of Congress Cataloging-in-Publication Data

Kutchins, Laurie.
Between towns : poems / by Laurie Kutchins.
ISBN 0-89672-296-1. — ISBN 0-89672-297-X (pbk.)
1. Wyoming—Poetry. I. title.
PS3561.U793B48 1992
811'.54—dc20 92-31518
CIP

93 94 95 96 97 98 99 00 01 / 9 8 7 6 5 4 3 2 1

Texas Tech University Press
Lubbock, Texas 79409-1037 USA

Acknowledgments

My thanks to the editors of the following publications where these poems, sometimes in different form, first appeared:

The Georgia Review: "Watching Great Grandma Bean Undress"
The Laurel Review: "A White Lie," "Ohio Nocturne"
New Voices: A 5-Year Anthology of College Prizes: "Black Lace"
Northern Lights: "Men Kick Stones When They Walk"
Painted Bride Quarterly: "The Same Road"
Ploughshares: "Daughter"
Southern Poetry Review: "Alchemy"
Tar River Poetry: "Settling"
Ucross: The First Ten Years: "Spring"
West Branch: "Full Circle"

I wish to thank the Pennsylvania Council on the Arts for a fellowship, and the MacDowell Colony and the Ucross Foundation for their generous support. Thanks also to the community of Ucross, Wyoming where a portion of this book was written.

I am deeply grateful to Miriam Garcia for her painting *Woman in the Clouds*, which appears on the jacket.

For Wyoming
and
for Rita

There are years that ask questions and years that answer.

Zora Neale Hurston

Foreword

One of the most significant changes in American poetry during the past two decades has been the nearly universal transformation of poetry book publishers into sweepstakes impresarios. Few poets think anymore in terms of earning publication; *winning* is the operative word, and many presses that consider poetry manuscripts have replaced traditional editorial practices with contests.

Today, publisher and poet alike inhabit a world of deadlines, entry fees, and long-shot odds that have changed what should be constructive contact between writer and editor into an impersonal game of chance. Gone are the days when poets paid their dues by earning recognition and the right to publish a book by first publishing widely in respected journals. Consumed by the promotion and management of their various contests, some press editors no longer read journals to discover new writers; and writers, in their turn, recognize the devalued role of journal publication. Both find it easier to stake everything on an annual lottery, where luck—always a factor—can overshadow hard work, accomplishment, and, arguably, even, merit.

Few presses have resisted the lure of the annual contest, and those succumbing to it have rarely modified the contest structure in any meaningful way. Notable among the latter group is Texas Tech University Press, where editor Judith Keeling has devised an idea that could restore integrity to the poetry publishing business. Highlighting the literary and not merely the marketing responsibilities of the press, poetry editor Walter McDonald actually reads literary journals and invites poets who impress him and who have not yet published a book to submit manuscripts for consideration by Texas Tech University Press.

Throughout the year, he reads from a list of approximately twenty journals. The list changes somewhat from year to year to increase coverage and always includes a wide range of respected quarterlies.

From his readings, McDonald selects about a dozen poets to whom Ms. Keeling issues invitations to submit manuscripts.

Elegantly simple, this approach calls to mind the days of hands-on editors who took an active interest in young writers and worked hard to promote new and promising talent. By choosing to do his own screening in the process of being an interested, engaged reader of poetry journals, McDonald removes the most onerous aspect of the contest system, the suffocating volume of submittals. Also eliminated are the entry fee, the contest deadline, and the boiler room of "slush" readers who stand between the editor or final judge and the larger body of work under consideration.

The positive outcome of this approach is amply illustrated by Laurie Kutchins's *Between Towns,* the choice resulting from McDonald's most recent reading and winnowing. Although it could easily be imagined as the "winner" of any national book prize, this collection might not have called enough attention to itself to keep the preliminary contest readers from pitching it into the rejection pile. Its strategies are subtle rather than flamboyant, reminding us that the best poems happen quietly.

Between Towns is unified by weather and landscape, and it is impossible to read this collection without feeling the openness of place and the lovely indifference of elements and animals going about their business. Inhabiting the same terrain as coyotes, aspens, wind, and snow, the narrator of these poems tries to perceive her place in a harsh but beautiful world. Central to her endeavor is an essential humility, a wonderful relinquishing of self to participate in something larger and more important than the individual ego.

Kutchins's cast of mind is decidedly metaphysical, and she holds her poise at the point of paradox, celebrating the stark opulence of a western environment. Hers is a desolate happiness characterized by an unflinching acceptance of herself as "a random form, / an uncamouflaged lump" (p. 3) in the world of hawks. Recognizing that there are "things I had to know / before my body," (p. 8) she is drawn toward moments of ineffable understanding, when the mysterious world calls her out of herself, though she is somewhat "afraid / to undress it or have it undress me." (p. 29)

Kutchins's focus is *between towns*, those out-of-the-way places where the noise of civilization hasn't obliterated the oracular voice of nature. And she is learning to feel connected and whole. Her quest is nowhere better stated than in the final section of "Shells":

> I look at the shells and the small imprints of spines in sandstone—
> they are only a slice of the story,
> but I touch them when I am lonely.
> I put them to my ear and listen,
> the land so still I believe it is breathing,
> though I cannot see it, change is all around me,
> no thing is static,
> the glaciers are moving imperceptibly in their beds,
> the sea is making decisions,
> rocks are blinking open; I hear their voices
> through broken walls, shells,
> a grandmother's whisper:
> trust your part.

The vital word here is *part*, *"trust your* part." The whole is much larger than any single person or thing, and Kutchins makes herself available to an almost visionary experience in which she celebrates her connectedness. Even the lowliest creatures have their place, and she looks in wonder at the mosquitoes she allows to drink from her and the tick that feeds secretly and then drops away, "her land pushed deeper / into the blood of me." (p. 45)

This is nothing less than the poetry of epiphany, something we have seen precious little of in our age. And it takes a courageous poet to deliver a message so at odds with our cynical, analytical world view. Filled with longing and joy, these poems remind us of a natural and spiritual ecology that can enrich our lives if we will let ourselves acknowledge it. No glib, quasireligious enthusiast, Kutchins leads along a way that is both difficult and dangerous; and she is a steady, reliable guide, her sure voice urging us on.

Laurie Kutchins is the real thing, a poet of substance and vision. Clearly, poetry for her is not a contest, and she is not playing games. Thanks to Walter McDonald's selction of this wonderful book, all who read it are the winners; and the luck is in the poems themselves.

Neal Bowers
Ames, Iowa

Contents

Full Circle

Coyote and Falling Star

Still Life with Hawks and Storms

This was a good day for hawks:
storms, then lulls, then more storms.
I envied their eyesight and grace.
They buck and float the blue wind, are one with it
the way I would like to be one with the impalpable circle
of the unconscious.

I want to know how their wings
hold and hoist them against the brutal currents,
rain slats, the rumbles of thunder,
how they join the immeasurable intelligence of cumulo-nimbi,
so at home under them.

The storms stirred up their prey,
rockchucks and mice scrambling in and out of rocks and scrubs.
The hawks circled and waited, vigilant.
Then dove, snatched, glided from sight.

Beneath their voracious shadows, I was a random form,
an uncamouflaged lump,
a mere whistle in their chain of being.
I was the least of their concerns.

Five storms crossed over today.
Five storms like dreams, four of which I've brought with me,
into the clearing.
The fifth being the most elusive, the most charged,
the darkest. The one you wait for.

Cows

I love how cows move across these meadows,
their heads held low and windward, to the wind,
the slow sway of rumps, thin tails, a long black line lumbering
toward the gates, the wagon and the broken
bales of hay. Though separately bulky
they seem to understand
the fluidity and power of a single line
and choose each time they move to move as one.
Walking they are as seamless as an oboist's breath.
This is why when she dies my mother claims
she's coming back as one of them.
At night, glancing up, still chewing, ready to calve,
the heifers' eyes stare into my flashlight,
their bodies impalpable, one with darkness.
So dark, I once heard one dying and did nothing.
In a squall their faces face it, huddled
in line along the fence,
and for this I love them, and for their breath rising
in the river trees on a February morning.
Come summer, the heifers' udders sag
like porcelain toilets, the calves grow fast and greedy,
their necks glistening or caked red
with mud. Walking, I've come upon their bodies
in every stage of decay —
that first bloat, eyes grabbed by magpies,
a pecked-out head, scrap of hide, deserted puzzles —
a bleaching never linear but scattered and strewn:
pelvis, shin, horn, broken narrative
of the last serious moan. I love their bones,
I bring them home.

Watching Great Grandma Bean Undress

She waits until she thinks I am sleeping
and perhaps I am, this feels so long ago,
but there at the musty edge of sleep
I hear her unmistakable shuffling:
size 5-N boots beakish and buttoned around
brittle, gooseneck ankles,
feet from a former century,
beechwood cane like a third foot
ticking over the tongue-in-groove farmhouse floor
the way her teeth grind
two worlds when she talks.

And there, out in the hall, after a long pause —
like the waiting that falls when a fish jumps
and the startled pond settles back
into itself — the slow turn of porcelain,
the bedroom door unbuttoned,
white fin of widening light and that first
uncertain odor of her entrance:
some rustbrown bottle kept for years
in a medicine chest is uncapped,
mingles with the pinch of rosemary
tucked like chew under her lip after supper.

Toward me she totters,
lumpy as a haystack in her black dress,
thinks I am sleeping
and keeps the room dark, the shadowed roots
of her fingers inching along the walls;
her face a tedious web of fears
and focus, careful of darkness, snags
in the braided rug, any fall

could be fatal;
self-conscious in her old-lady noises,
she trolls toward sleep and my body
still young and new breasted
breathing and sleeping in the other half
of her wide bed. I watch
through a keyhole in the quilt.

Leaning against the nightstand, she
steadies herself, works the dress off
step by step, birdnest hair matted down.
Now she is all slips and straps,
rusty hinges hugging an old barn against the dead
weight of winter.
Then these go.

I want to shutter myself against her
nakedness, but even now she is there,
moley and white as birchbark,
hairless in the shrunken
fork of her crotch,
she and her daughter and her daughter
and her daughter who is me
lingering in this one body.

When she lowers herself slowly into bed
beside me, her bones cranking out
small hooks of anger at being wakened,
an old boot odor rises up
from under those magnificent fallen breasts,
those ancient sucked-out moons.

The Wind

All my life I have known the wind, all my life it has hovered close
pushing back the gates, coming and going,
surely someone's breath along my collarbone.
Bodiless, its mission is to delight in my body.
On summer afternoons it slips up the sleeves of my blouse, my skirt flares,
it dabbles and plays about the nipples, rouses them
into pimpled delirious berries.
It swishes through my hair as through water and a swan's neck.
When I am walking windward at the end of winter and leaning into it,
the wind flutters along my tongue carrying twig-stuff and leaf-crust,
building its gnarled nest in my lungs,
reclaiming the abandoned nest it once wedged in my fallopian crook.
All my life the wind has been pushing and pulling me
to and from the cardinal points, bestowing me with indecisions,
with restlessness and nocturnal wandering,
luring me into places I might not otherwise go,
tugging at me, overturning all the nests everywhere trying to get it right,
a message with no messenger.

Though no one has told me this, I know the wind was there
shaking the windows and bed when I was conceived,
my mother frightened by the sound of me coming,
my father tossing under the covers, wandering the house,
touching the latches.
Though no one has told me, the wind was there at the birth table,
navigating, coaxing my nostrils,
cutting me loose from the fluid outlet.
Yes I am certain the wind was there,
it rubbed its sadness into my shoulders,
sucked on my mysterious fingers,

it sifted its dust into my cheeks and eyes,
flushed its trembling and its tenacity into my larynx,
its larva of anger under my glands.
I am certain the wind knew when I would come,
it wrestled me into April and May,
it ushered me just as it will when it is ready for me to die.
I heard the wind bending the lilacs, ringing white fragrant bells,
it rattled the porch swing where my mother waited
turning the pages of magazines,
it whistled in my father's teeth as he went out
late that night to start the car,
I heard it bending down to meet me,
an ear, a pair of lips
brushing past the round of a hill, I heard
the wind briefly between doorways
delivering its urgent message,
things I had to know
before my body.

Coyote and Falling Star

Walking the unlit path from the barn I am happy, so convinced am I
there is another world to which this one is but a subset.
I am the noisiest thing around: when I stop,
inhale and look round,
the snow-scrunching, wool-rubbing sound of me — my slim
companion —
also stops, jumps into my pockets,
holds her breath and waits:
silence, yes, is the faithful lull,
the ultimate tongue-lick, the first love.

And if I stopped for long enough would the sound of me die?

It is so dark I cannot see myself — hearing is everything.
Which world am I standing in,
suddenly lost under hayrolls of stars?

I think then of the births and deaths at the tips of me.
The bloated ewe crippled up, poisoned, pulled down
by dead triplets in her.
In her eyes the dark, intricate animal pain
getting ready.
The dog that lapped up the last of her blood on the shed floor.
The calf that was coming backwards,
Les's long hands sliding along its hind legs, reaching,

the snapped cord,
the last breath before a first ever arrived,
a black head drowned in uterus juice.

Is this death, when a pair of nostrils kick
but never grip dry air?

How long until there's a small skull on the hill,
the wind whittling white holes?
And farther, a thin dragged hind bone
laced with gnawings.

I live so lazily, convinced of that other world.
But it's all here: nothing more, nothing less
than five seconds of silence lost,
a full revolution of breath
and far off, out of nowhere
a coyote —
a pure sound ending all thoughts, luring my eyes upward
where a star,
an old crippled star, its proud tail flaring as it staggers down,
plunges into the opened throat.

Spring

At the bar, Bob tells me that women make the best lambers.
A woman, he says, knows something a man doesn't
about the pain. Something she doesn't need to put words to,
a thing she carries in her fingers.
I like the way he says woman —
it feels like someone has let go
in my spine a small balloon filled with helium
and it is drifting neckward.

I am walking the soft snowless spines of the shale hills,
gathering bones, rocks, wind, a nest blown down,
a pair of antlers rubbed off only hours ago,
gathering everything into my arms.
I am seeing and smelling the intricate green
of what is yet to come.
It is March and I feel it
in the back of my neck, woman, the way he says it,
with envy and a secret ache.

I hold the ewe's head while Bob reaches inside,
turns the backwards lamb and pulls.
Blindness and shock of initial light.
He tickles the nostrils with a quill of last year's grass
drained of green and flattened from snow:
quivers of breath.
He massages and shapes its glistening legs
as if he were fluffing the ribbons on a package.

Bob holds the soundless ewe's head while I pack a mound
of hay under its bloat, and reach
inside, up past my elbow to feel

the others in there,
the first one already standing alone, shivering in real air,
opening its eyes, bleating and searching
and shaking the birth from its ears.

Weather

I am at home where weather is a big deal.
I belong in the flurry of nerves, in the wire and talk
when the front veers away from the forecaster's stick on the map —
guaranteeing he'll be sheepish the next day —
and comes slithering toward us, unexpected snake
of sleet, snow, squall, hail, rain, lightning, wind, blizzard.
I am at home where weather is the active link.

I am at home with year-round chains and blizzard kits.
Where skilled fingers fiddle with dials,
and ears once frost-nipped perk, mark the forecast
out of the chatter, jukebox, and pool-table din
like a woman plucking an arrow tip out of a ridgetop of stones.

It's March and it's snowing, and this is not the end of it.
At the bar, the ranchers stand around, warming up, checking in.
They are lambing and calving, day and night,
weather is either an intimate friend, nurse, or albatross.
They warm their hands on steamy coffee,
their lips on dry cigarettes,
they smell of smoke and wet wool, of snow and wind and uterine
    blood.
Outside their trucks idle, windshields and windows whitening
like old men's shoulders, heeler dogs curled on seats
in snow-cocoons, waiting.

I am at home anywhere men and women are telling weather stories.
The time when a single gust tossed a dog in its doghouse
out of the yard.
The blizzard of '84 when things modern shut down for days,
the livestock stuck under snow,
the storm when a pregnant woman left her car in search of gas,

wasn't found until the clearing, days later,
frozen against a pumping oil pump.
The Thanksgiving storm of '79 when stranded travelers
took up every inch of church in the towns between
Cheyenne and Sheridan.
The time when Horse, laying fence, trapped his thumb between wire,
stood there under the January sun hoping someone would come,
and by dusk whacked his thumb off
to get home before the dark froze him
stiff as a fence post.
The time when on a roundup the cows were deliberately turned loose
in a torrent because lightning is drawn to things in huddles.
I am at home in these stories.

It's May and it's snowing wet horizontal snow, and this is not the end
of it.
The ranchers are up all hours, feeding and counting their stock,
standing around, warming their lungs, waiting it out.
The school bus brings the children home early.
I belong where towns end, the highways leading out
have metal gates across them
and twelve-foot snow fences hug the roads.
I am at home where root cellars and windows are left unlocked
and a rope is strung between the house and barn.
I am at home where weather is a parental voice I still listen for.

The Same Road

Where the house blurred into the windbreak
of half-grown trees, we turned back to wave,
certain she'd still be there.
My sister and I let go our brother's hand;
we laid our books in the cold gravel
of Poison Spider Road, packed stones to keep the wind
from rustling the homework into barbed wire
hours west of us,
our arms flapping with a keen knowledge of the mother.

She waited at the window, I believed, solely for us,
her breath a white knot where it touched the glass,
a sweater slung over her shoulder.
I willed we'd find her in the window when we turned,
but in truth, wind and the slur of stones had pushed us
too far down that road to see her, or her us:
the house small as a latch on the sage flats
and getting smaller.

I was her daughter: into dry snow-scatter I drifted
and the seeds of her longing settled deep
in the reddened folds of my ears.
That's how I've come to believe the end of winter
is the longest wait, a weight that kills the calves,
snaps hope from the limbs and keeps the cottonwood
creaking in the yard. When finally it comes,

spring is a parting, a slow journey
begun in the dark bud-hard ground, unseen,
accomplished in its own time.

Meanwhile, it pressed her face to the window,
furrowed and torn as if she were also following
the migration of something far beyond us
on the same road.

Men Kick Stones When They Walk

One night, waking me, the scuffle
of wind at the water pump,
lifting and lowering the arm
at the rusted hinge. Wind
harnessed in the cottonwoods
groaning down by the vacant bunkhouse,
a sound I half-dreamed
was Wally, whiskied and cussing
in his joints, come back for chores
after a night trip to town,
his good eye lost in its eye blood.
Wind scraping the voices
of my parents, so hushed
in the cold of the kitchen
it seemed they were sleeping.
But there, clearly now,
a muscular stubborn murmur,
the cinched hollow sound I would hear
Dad make deep in the slope
of his throat each time he'd
stoop to lug the carcasses
at the end of winter.
I lay there deciphering
the sounds the dark gathered
in my ears, wind slapping the house
and Dad asking: *still your lover?*
A phrase set loose and lost
in the open space between hunch
and consolation.
And when the wind eased
I heard the thin walls hold
my mother's sighing, small and pinched

as a whistle through a clothespin,
a cold cheek pressed to the sop
of yolk and white in her apron,
chapping that face forever.

* * *

Mornings I liked best
in the small dark kitchen,
the sun still climbing
to the top of Crow Heart Butte
where once — as Dad could tell it
so much better than the books —
the kind-hearted chief Washakie
had speared, stolen, stick-fired
and swallowed the glistening
black heart of the Crow.
And so, the only light was
the sometimes oil lamp
at the long pine table
and the mercy of the wood stove
belching its first heat and smoke
and orange stars into the chilly room.
And her there working the griddle,
manly in her ranch clothes, apron untied,
hair in her way, the way I liked it best,
drowsy and not yet pinned up.

She poured scalded milk
into a metal cup, scooped a dollop
of stiff cream on top to hold the steam in.
My tongue turned numb and the cup

toasted my fingers holy.
Toes crimped in the outgrown boots
thumping against the nook bench.
Moon scrunched down in sagebrush
like the shuddering white butt
of a struck antelope.
And soon the November sound
of the men — Dad, Wally, and Steve
boot-kicking the cold
between shed and house, chores and breakfast.
Then the cluck of worn-down heels
in the mud room,
hats lassoed over the elk rack,
three frozen thumb-nips at my ears
as they eased their stiff bodies
down to a hot meal.
She'd have it ready but wouldn't sit
until they'd started in on seconds:
griddle toast, pork rind, apple butter,
fried eggs with yolks broken,
Tabasco and jalepenos for Wally
who never told the same story twice
about his glass eye.
The sun would avalanche
the close side of the butte,
blaze the table forks, and outside
a circle of stones at the pump
was recast in the light,

ruddy and dazzling as the oranges
Steve would send dead-winter
from Arizona.

* * *

It seemed as if the weather controlled them,
and it was always changing. Dad said
he could feel a storm in his knees;
I could feel it in the way they talked
of the cold, the truck that needed tires
and the Tuesday blizzard sulking
over the tops of the Wind Rivers.
Wally and Steve saying they ought
to be heading south soon,
on down to Flagstaff,
Dad pinching his cigarette, saying
hard to believe how the year's
getting on and we would manage.
I could feel it when their *so longs*
brushed the shadows in my ears,
in how far away the horizon leaned
afterwards, and in her hard glance
down to a pine gnarl in the floor.
And in a silence
locked in each of them
like the straight dirt road
into town.

Some talk I'd forget
and some was a kind of wide open
I'd want to ride out of for good,

but why did that kind stay with me,
loyal and fierce as the chapped
handshake of the wind down Bull Lake,
or the black shriek of water
when I broke through
thin ice, losing my hat to an ocean?
Their voices stayed with me, like the way
men kick stones when they walk,
boot tips pointing toward timberline,
some waiting country high up and pure,
cirques where the snow is constant.

A White Lie

For the first time ever, it is snowing
in Midland, Texas. I am seven years old,
telling the earliest lie I remember
to Miss White, my second grade teacher,
her lips mysterious and perfectly red.
My lips quiver, my words nervous at their work.
I want to go out beyond the school windows,
our huge paper snowflakes pressed in every pane;
I want to wander across the enormous lawn, halfway out
into the unmarked center of snow,
touch its cold vocabulary, and turn,

and look back at where I've come,
my tracks vanishing like turtles in the morning,
and smile at how small school is,
how real, for once, the snow in the window
suddenly seems.

I'm telling a lie about leaving
books in a bike basket.
As I speak I believe my voice in the grayness
filling with snow
in the understories of my eyes:
if the intention is good,
if the intention is the intention.
I no longer know what it is I am saying
but the words fall from my tongue and turn
into swans, and then

I step lightly out
of that classroom into the pure white
world of the lie because there was always
this desire and something
about leaving something behind.

Alchemy

Where it is getting dark, the trees are turning
bold and dreamy.
I am pedaling a slow rusting bicycle,
riding farther than before,
into the deep green eye
of evening.

The time we create is time lost.

A girl in a screened gazebo is painting her first picture.

She should be reading history lessons or scripture
but the words whisper
touch me.

Her lips and fingers
doused with the dropped seeds
of light.

It is a pastoral she is making:
layers of dung, sod, green to golden grasses,
grains cut and stacked,
grains burning,

milk cows whose tongues have awakened
to nurse the field-cud

brought back from the terraced soup
of their bodies.

It is the clicking of wind through wheel spokes.

A sound to which the cows lift their dull eyes,
a movement the foreground holds, loses
among the flicker of leaves
darkening under the undulant trees.

I know this girl, both of us traveling
away from the factual dusk,
making the other
out of desire.

What swarms in us is a sensual distance—
how far we must go
not to hear it, the tower bell,
the real one,
turning the hour.

Black Lace

This

Coming home from the river in the dusk of day, I hear it
there in the uncut grass,
that indolent grinding,

warm wind breathing on the backs of stones.
I hear it in the clipped stars that tumble and catch
in the wings of crickets.

I've never known where it comes from, where it goes
when it goes, I drift after it,
my voice calling to the far edge of the field:
who are you
graceful and noisy in your grace?

Sometimes it's how the air turns suddenly thick,
droops like limbs of ready pears, gritty
mouth-harps of late summer;

sometimes when it wakes me and I can't tell
if it's peepers or leaves pelting the walk,
I come so close but am afraid
to undress it, or have it
undress me:

this might not be what I think,
this might be, exactly.

Meetings

Invisible, the stray cat meowing at the door this morning,
has a new gash across his nose.
His white tail floats across my shins
as I place his scraps on the snow.
His comings and goings have nothing to do with the wild geese
honking overhead,
shaking the night out of their wings.

* * *

There are gashes in the cottonwoods along the river,
not fresh like Invisible's gash, but old ones,
substantial and deep.
A giants' hands shredded their bark like a napkin at a picnic —
a mindless, nervous gesture.
I touch the hard white inner skins,
gently, as if I were bathing an old man's shoulders,
listening to the stories of the scars.

* * *

Something in the morning air is holding me, daring me to go inside.
It pulls my knees into the snow, tickles me,
insists I come in contact
with frost tips on a barbed wire fence,
bird arrows carved over a hundred years ago
by a Crow warrior who had his own names for the past.
These are his names melting into my hand.

* * *

I scare a porcupine as far up into a tree as it can climb
before its own fear pulls it back to me.
It quills into a relentless nest, a camouflage

within a camouflage.
We stare across the cold at one another.
Only a nostril twitches.

* * *

At the convergence of three creeks I stop, the ice too thin
to trust a crossing.
The ice makes a vast, hollow sound. A ripping open.
Someone is here demolishing an old settlement, layer by layer.
Someone is tiptoeing across,
passing through walls
to greet me,
love me.

How Crazy Woman Canyon Got Its Name

1. The Sioux Indian Woman

Wind. I carry an infant of wind in my arms.
I carry a branch on my back,
fat greying braid,
a thing to burn and warn you.
Eyes to the ground, I lay my ear on the red stone.
This is how I know
you and I are close.
You are the slow imperceptible slips
of grass,
veins of butterflies,
the hungry ghost dance of my arms.

Please recognize me.
I am no longer young.
Sorrow has gouged its intricate canyons
in my skin,
my eyes are the dark holes in the cottonwood tree
where lightning grounded.
Know me as the one who held you when you wandered,
when you wanted holding.
The one who pulled the hide,
threaded the moccasins
for your change of worlds.

Come close.
I have something to tell you:
The third moon has stolen your last seed
from my body.
I have something to tell you: you are my husband
but also my child

for didn't I give birth to you
when I placed the red made of burnt clay
across your face,
when I smelled your blood and semen
on the fingers of the wind?

Each time I come here, the others follow and find me.
They tug at my arms, pull me away
but each time I return.
Is it the wind in the canyon walls
I follow
or the silent thirst of the doe
edging down among long fragile grass?

Come close. Take me in your arms.
Breathe into my openings
and enter me,
make love to my failure.
When you go, go
slowly,
slow as at dusk the light leaves the land.

2. The Pioneer Woman

Last Monday out where the canyon begins, past the rim
of wagons I wandered out — it was May and a whiff of wild lilac
tugged at me like my own child at my sleeve
and I wandered into the lost perfume   into the wind
holding the first and last promise of home,
lilacs and lace and rain swaying in an open window —
how long ago was it I wandered
out past wheel spokes and flapping canvas

past the children playing ghosts in the smoke of our circle
past the greasewood of the cooking fires, the clatter of iron at dusk
past the dust on the oxen's backs, the thirst in their hooves
past the men sun caked and weary under the eyes
and the women leathering under bonnets and thinking here
was enough water to wash,
thinking I was the cool dark throat of an owl
thinking I was the curious slit in nothingness
thinking past the rim of my existence I wandered out
out to where the vanishing place begins.
Soon it got dark, the stars thickened over me like a placenta
and I thought I heard her singing
and I thought I heard my name flickering out of the firelight,
fluttering up to the stars, I thought I heard my children's weeping
and my husband, the rub of his knife upon a wheel.
Was this my voice saying *here, here?*
How long ago was Monday? — a moment, a century, or a year —
there is a silence past the mindless turnips of wind
there is a brilliance like a cuff link on a stone
there is a snowflake in a bottle, a lunacy to calendar time.
A woman knows the first sadness,
in turn, she is its keeper and its ears.

Bloodroot

I recognize the smell of thunder gathering
over the scrub sage, the distance I am driving towards.
Beside me my sister flicks the dial off,
not getting anything but static and country.
She falls asleep, her throat tipped
like a baby bird swallowing seed grains.
I watch her mouth, which looks like mine, opening

toward the outcrops and night storms between towns.
Out there are the immense questions of our past,
curled in fossils from an ocean,
the inarticulate bones of childhood,
questions I'm looking for a way to ask.
They brush against us in the wind, will outlast the mesas,
the bouldered creeks teased by storms.

They come that close — in what blooms ahead,
the eyes of antelope, white necks raised,
grazing in the cusp of our headlights.
How much later I will awaken to find
a bloodroot on my tongue,
white and exquisite in its blossom,
poisonous in the root ends.
And a child's hand pressed over my mouth.

Bones

Thinking of my father's bones, I know that I have inherited
the white arthritic ache of him,
I have inherited the blonde alluvium that carries my shame
into my marrow, the crevasse where he hurls things
that never climb back out. I lean and peer
down the long slide of bones,
and I know nothing but the desire to be separate.

I wish that I'd been born instead along the hollow
wing bones of an owl, the wind making its home upon my clavicle.
I want the wind to reshape my bones
as it does the bones of snow, rocks, lightning.
My father's bones ache and harden. He refuses a burial.
I want my bones to soften, flow and illuminate the landscape
when I am old.
What might I be then, when the glacial slice
of his life has long since left me?

My father knows the earth's past, how its bones become air,
metamorphic slate and raw energy.
High upon the jagged mountain he traces
the spine of a fish.
Deep in the rock he finds carcasses of stars,
the cheekbones of winter, old footprints of wind.
He knows bones turn beneath us, softening
into soupy fuels.
But he has no memory of his own, and I am left looking

for a boy lost among the ministers' voices,
his loneliness among sisters,
the roughage of unloved bones.

I see him dying among snow.
He'll wander out alone some long night onto his land,
taking nothing but the dark
melodies of Mahler, the hard white road home.
Stopping to rest, his eyes and mouth open,
he'll fill with snow.

Bone of the dutiful daughter, bone of wind
upon the cold tongue of road,
bone of Mahler that carries my father out,
bone of outgrown shame and sorrow,
bone of the moon inside the mountain,
bone of the buffalo in the Fire Hole River gathering light and air,
bone of the snow fleck on his wristbone,
bone where the soul sleeps and waits:
I am the one to burn them.

Shells

1.

In an arid place I bend to pluck a small coiled shell from the trail.
Proof there was an ocean here. I hold it in my palm
like a one-winged butterfly, as if it were alive.
I lift my sunglasses to examine its ridges, fossilized lines
finer than those on the topo map in my pocket.
How long has this shell waited for someone to come along
and lift it from its cradle,
earth, how long has it waited for the touch
of my fingertips?

The shell is as primitive
and elegant as the face of an old woman
who has spent her life among rocks and dry wind.
The face I am going to become.

Dusk comes behind a curtain of thin rain.
I walk the ridge, touching the shell in my pocket,
trying to imagine this land as the floor of an ocean.
I breathe the rain smell on the sage, its pungence
stronger than the rain itself.
I am part of the circular air
where shadows lengthen along dry creeks,
where old snow trickles then roars seaward,
always seaward.

2.

Easter Sunday: Rita and I walk as far out on the tip
of the cape as we can go.
Ellie my dog races back and forth on the sand
chasing the waves as they gather, foam, crest, and disperse
always a little ahead of her.
She yips and spins, work to be done,
trying to herd the waves like sheep.

The odor of the sea is new to me,
the salt on my tongue not the salt of my own body,
the fine sand the sea winds lift from the earth and brush into my ears,
the colors of the fishing village, the beach, boats, sky —
everything blue, white, unfamiliar.

But the ocean is a loneliness I recognize,
an open stretch
in which I can see what is coming
long before it arrives.

Broken, the shells scuttle in,
wrap themselves in foam at my feet.
I pick them up, finger their smooth shapes
trying to piece one together.

I hold the inner spiral of a conch shell,
an ear from the underworld.
If I put it back, how many times will it trundle again to land,
dry, weather, then swirl back into the sea
looking for its lost body?

3.

Our hair windblown, Rita and I walk the shoreline for hours,
our scalps, shins and teeth caked with sand grit,
our voices turned toward the Atlantic.

There is a language we share whether it comes to us in words
or in silence.

There is a language we share, our mothers
turned out of Europe as children.
They crossed the Atlantic on freight ships
under the winter stars,
ocean and sky one dark sandwich,
odors of fish and waves and vomit,
finger holes in their mothers' woven shawls, our grandmothers
younger than we are now.
The slap of the waves against the dock,
sea legs on Ellis Island, papers, letters,
the slap of a new language in their ears,
the shame of the first language slipping back
forever under their tongues.

I gaze across the stiff sea wind and the blur of waves
into the silence that is the past and the future.
A flock of gulls flutter up from the sand,
cry their screeching cry

and drift far out beyond that place in the sea
where the waves begin to form
and come in again.

I follow the slow curvature of the earth,
beyond this sea our mothers crossed
hoping to find that part of me,
the feminine line buried and burned there.

I put the shell to my ear.
I have no locket, no swirl of hair, no letters of grandmothers.
Their voices are the missing pieces,
the difference between a story and none,
the Chanukah candles burning,
a swinging bridge in the Black Forest,
the yellow stars that told them it was time.

4.

There are shells I carry with me,
in pockets or in purses that glide on the electrical ramps,
under the lamps of instant x-rays in airports
where an official woman looks down into them,
tightens her brow, nods her head for me to pass.
She does not know that she is looking into the past,
her eyes scanning the mollusks, corals,

brachiopods, trilobites and ancient scraps,
smoothed or pocked, whole or broken in rocks
that once formed the sandy floor of the Sundance Sea.

I look at the shells and the small imprints of spines
in sandstone —
they are only a slice of the story,
but I touch them when I am lonely.
I put them to my ear and listen,
the land so still I believe it is breathing,
though I cannot see it, change is all around me,
no thing is static,
the glaciers are moving imperceptibly in their beds,
the sea is making decisions,
rocks are blinking open; I hear their voices
through broken walls, shells,
a grandmother's whisper:

trust your part.

Cynthia's Forsythia

For when the moon has outgrown the sky and gone,
and rain is falling on the fields like hair across a sleeping face,
I think of that forsythia in bloom and nothing else,
nothing that doesn't twist away from

or back to the wild hedge, wild yellow boundary
between the things I can touch and things I can't,
colorful scream of birth out of numbness,
a fragrance floating through my sleep.

And I know that it is Cynthia's forsythia I miss
and all that this forsythia is:
more than the moonlight wandering
into the lips of her tulips,

more than the morning glories that gloriously creep
along the trellis and the string,
more than the fox I found beneath the bloom,
its paw mangled in the trap some hunter abandoned

or forgot before he died.
The dead especially deserve to be free.
I touch its paw when I release it,
delicate bones of an old, now shapeless, sadness.

Morning After a Week of Storms

Sitting outside I hear again the low hot hum of the mated
hummingbirds at the feeder, drawn back to the brilliant
red orb of sugar water I have prepared for them.
Out of the washed air they dart, unannounced duet
of flits, they nuzzle and dip their dainty
frenetic beaks into the sweet
scarlet nectar, glistening liquid sex
in a plastic globe they zip out of nowhere for; their wings
flutter so fast they are invisible; their bodies
hum vibratos, a flurry of *vvvvvvvvv*'s
coming together, the female a fresh streak of green, the male
a greedy glint of red, yellow, and green, both of them
daring a fleet of orgasmic sips
around my ears.
In the clearing
the storms have dropped white seedlings
over the mountains and drifted on
to another valley. So happy am I in the sunlight
I let the blue flies rehearse on my white wrists,
I let a female mosquito or two
just hatched, come home,
offspring of some that fed from me last summer,
legs long and delicate, wings
elegant as a bridal net, and for the first time
I don't despise them, I envy
their bellies translucent,
bloated and blood-fat
from lovers.

Walk in Tick Season

The tick that wanders up my leg,
skirting the bloodless knee and following the cool
hidden tunnel of my trousers,
has but one thing on her mind.
She's looking for a meal, a place to moisten
her throat, a quiet bed to settle down and hide
her head from the hard sun.
She would like to find the ravine behind my ear,
the oils in my hair, or the shade
under the rub of my arm.
Just a moment ago, with legs
as determined as the talons of the hawk
that plucked a rabbit swiftly into the sky,
she leapt from a stalk of sagebrush
onto my boot as I brushed by. She is crawling
as lightly as the morning breeze
on my skin, the vast space
that makes her think she goes unnoticed.
She carries the grey-green blush of the sage,
its pungency when a droplet falls,
engorged, from a passing cloud.
Once she finds her place,
she will sip and sleep and ride
the freight of my body
until she falls off, oblivious and bloated,
her land pushed deeper
into the blood of me.

Invertebrate Drift

Boneless, they carry the two huge kidneys of night.
Out of snowmelt, morainal slush
seeping out of the ancient glands of glaciers, into streams
they drift. In the currents that pull them,
they drown their past.

Inexplicably, they leave miniscule messages in unopened egg sacs,
in inlets on the undersides of rocks,
in gooey algae, in the black alluvial stuff—
unfinished crossword puzzles for biologists.

Untraced, they abandon their hidden cities, drift out alone.
Using the stars as eyes they wiggle deeper
into the dark wet privacy of the unconscious,
the earth's nomadic tongues.

While somewhere a man packs up his saxophone and goes home,
while somewhere a waitress counts out her tips,
folds them into a napkin, hails a cab and goes home,
they drift.

While somewhere a trucker burns his brakes,
diesels up, makes a phone call he regrets in his spine,
the road dead
a long stretch ahead of him,
they drift.

While somewhere a woman awakens,
not because her phone is ringing
not because the baby screams to be nursed and silenced,
or the unborn one is navigating its moonless kayak,
or the lonely ovule migrates down her blood,

but awakens for no known reason,
they drift;

while she watches her face in the kitchen window,
remembers a water dream,
sips a glass of whiskey,
then a glass of milk,
they drift.

While somewhere a coyote and a horned owl prey separately
on the carcass of a fawn, hurled into the ditch grass
by a passing truck,
they drift.

While somewhere a star drops into unmeasured darkness,
they drift.

While closer a bear lifts her nose in the hawthorn thicket,
sniffs the fishy air, smells nothing she knows as fear
and drifts back into drowsiness,
they drift.

While the trout twitch with the current
huddled and resting between stones,
while the stones release what leaves them
and the fishermen sleep
huddled and breathing under western stars,
their mouths settled and open, lungs sipping the glacial air,
while their pickups glisten
like immense humps of slow-grazing buffalo,
in the middle of the night,
they drift.

Ghosts

Late in the night
through the grid pores of the screen
they urge me. Curious
they come close
and lumpy against me, their fear
pressed over my stomach
like a pregnancy
of wet sand.

Outside I drift
in a white nightdress, my dead breasts
cold in the nipples,
my toes sponging the apple grass
the late ooze
of the field out back,
and I begin to see
that nothing stops
or ends, though it pretends to
when we are static.

See how the willow shags
are shooing the wind
into the sheds, clairvoyant hands
cup the moon as it dilates,
opens around me,
see how the crickets warble
in their knees the intangible
textures of mileage
as one last traveller
whisks along the highway.

Black Lace

On the last of those moves
I lost the pair of black lace panties
he'd given me. In one of those motels
we came to, damp, irritable, hungry,
on the outskirts of the granary towns.
Probably they just got stuck down at the frame
of the bed where the sheets curve and tuck
under the mattress like fast water
sealing its dark envelope.
That lapse in a poorly-made bed
where the shadows hide things for a long time.

I can't think of any other explanation.
How we rushed around those green curtained rooms
those mornings we slept until checkout. It was still raining
and the thought of more rain, wet road,
wipers squeaking across the windshield,
made us not want to go anywhere.
Or care where we stopped over.

Through the transient landscape of sex I wore them.
I wanted to know he still wanted me.
I wanted to lose everything I owned
in my body and feel as though I had arrived
at no other place than the purely
physical moment
which was always gypsying on
to someplace else where the meals were better.

I wonder where I left them,
which room, which night of our caravan
across the country. And how long it took

before some cabin maid found them
flattened against the bed like a sock
on the wire matting of a public dryer;
hooked her thumbs through the scanty leg holes
and stretched them across the silence
of her hips to see if they might fit
into some other life,
a life where entirely different things
are lost and not meant to be gotten back.

Full Circle

Settling

The workmen across the road were stripping the old farmhouse.
All afternoon as I unpacked
I heard their scrape-scrape-scraping,
their careful shifting of ladders from east to south to west.
They laid white tarps over the hedges
like a linen table service for the finches
that looked on and twittered in the sugar maples
already starting to change.
I respected the workers' diligence,
the way they broke only for coffee and lunch
and even at that kept it short.
Their sense of purpose welcomed me,
although I think I would have preferred
they left that place alone. I'd lived here three days
and the rain-battered stare of the abandoned house
out my window was already turning
into some kind of old-lady friend.

Mid-afternoon my telephone rang for the first time.
I tried to picture him, still back in California,
standing at a pay phone on a street I knew,
breathing that *dim-sum* air, ginger and garlic,
the bougainvillea in bloom
and the hills coming back to green.
I remembered the difference in time.
But I couldn't see him.
Where are you, I asked, and meant it.
I'm sorry, he whispered mid-sentence,
then hung up. Later, after the workmen had gone,
and the last funnel of sunlight exploded

on their ladders, the phone rang again.
This time there was no voice, only meandering static —
frayed wings trapped in the power lines.
I thought, maybe it was the old house calling.
The odd silence I loved, knowing
I was its other half.

River in Winter

It's here, under the surface hush.

Knocking inside the cellar pipes, keeping me warm.
Lost in the walls, it floats through the sleeves of mice, keeping me
awake.
It tunnels into the large nights.

Its give is the deepest resistance.

I put my face to the window: that man on the other side
is trying to tell me something

something I will need to take with me,
but his voice freezes and clings to the glass, where our faces blur,

and all I hear is the thudding
of stunned blood,
hands practicing an alphabet underwater.

When he went away I stood on the ice, which is only a skin,
not a true terrain. I looked up:
there were the stars, tiny, immutable towns in the distance —

and then it cracked, not under me but off to one side.
It was a muffled scream, a long denial
rooting out into the night air —

I looked up: the stars had pulled closer.

The snow, in its first falling, is giddy and delicate.
It is the briefest kind of freedom,
and like love, a journey indifferent to endings or source.

It flutters down to the river and disappears.
It flutters down to itself and the river disappears,

its movement is what I long for when it stops.

Sometimes when the ice severs its grip, out of the breakage
ragged, beautiful edges form

and out of the edges, the underside that holds me
sends a message:

let go let go

the desire to become
as one w/ nature, feeling
close but not quite

Woman Dressing

The woman dresses quickly to cover herself from the cold.
It's the time of year when the hardest thing is to let go
of the shadowed heat the body makes for itself
under the dark quilts. It is hard to leave at any hour
in winter when the cold hangs on,
clamping its icicle teeth around the eaves,
and moonlight falls through the windows and radiator slats,
trying to warm itself.
This hour before the delivery boy upstairs patters swiftly
across the bare floor to start his shower.
If you are awake, this frozen hour is a silence
so strong you hear the particles construct the minutes,
you hear the road gathering the privacy
of animals that cross, like blowing snow,
slow and safe under the moon.

Like a letter pulled carefully from an envelope, the woman
eases away from the sleeping man
in the other half of the bed.
She shivers over him, sculpts the quilts
along his back and shoulders to leave him
the lingering smoke of her body.
She sees his eyelids flutter, as if birds were migrating under them,
his dreams restless in his skin.

Even out of bed she feels his breathing pull her
under like a wave. Sometimes she imagines drowning,
drifting out and vanishing like a floating candle.
She touches the skin over the gnarled highways of blood

where her breasts come together,
and wonders where a dream goes when it shudders out
of the body and wanders back into the wintry air.

Before the light rises, before the moon drops into the ridge of firs,
she is going to drive somewhere. Where she doesn't know,
but there are good roads and farmhouses she can pass,
wondering if someone lying awake in a room hears her.
Maybe she will stop to watch the ice drifting,
animals feeding on the muscle of the river. Or she can stop
at the cafe by the highway to warm up.
If she feels like it, after that, she'll keep going, or circle back
before he wakes and knows she's gone.
She leaves a few of the buttons open,
her fingers clumsy with cold.

Summer Dawn

I am awake for no reason.
At the window. On the porch.
The moon is a beautiful ear slipping a question
in slippery whispers into the aspens.
I cannot hear it, but I see it,
all of it, and it is already
three-quarters gone.

It is not possible to know. I press
my palms against my breasts:
they are swollen,
milkless,
full of hills on the insides.

Today is a seedling
drifting under the earth.

I think of the animals drifting
so close my body senses them,
so close

surely they smell me,
their necks rising from the grass.

This is not easy,
this darkness putting forth
such light.

Across the valley I count
the lights of the original ranches, so few,
when my breath reaches them
they shiver
like flame vanishing down a match.

The dust is asleep on the road,
the moon gone under
a pink rim.
And now I hear a bird begin to sing in its sleep,
nudging a dream out of someone
waking in a city, far away,
bringing it home to me
at last.

Night Bird

After dark, the red bird in the bare tree near my window
still sings. Its song was the first thing
I awakened to this morning
before dawn, before I remembered the unknown
twitching in the inner hide of me,
small red tongue in my womb
singing back to the bird.
And it is the last thing I hear
as the night comes back, drapes its long
outgrown winter cloak
carefully across my house.

A cold rain is falling,
the cloak glistens like a season
afraid to glide out
and still the bird
is singing.
How do I know if it remembers
this morning?
I doubt the bird knows the future any better
than I do. It simply sings,
throat opened, song flung
to the out there that goes,
to the in here throbbing on a branch
of liquid dark —
this night *this* bird

Poems to the Quaking Aspen

1.

Each evening, I walk down to you to listen.
Your youngest
who were too young to know me
last summer,
now hover about my face and sing to me.
They are just learning to sing with their small green skirts
flapping on the updrafts,
quivering and lifting their song
toward the elders;
with leaflets so perfect I hesitate
to touch them.

Their sapling bark—
soft as first velvet on the antlers
of the elk who will wait
until I have gone
to come down,
rub their secret necks
against you, and feed.

2.

Though I do not completely belong,
I meander and bend among your whispers.
I embrace the smell of summer in your house.
You are more alive to me

you who understand things
about fear
I am afraid to learn.

What's here?
Chartreuse eyes, undersides of voices.
Is it the porcupine waiting for nightfall
to lift your dead,
or the bear nosing a carcass,
or the great horned owl who makes its night watch
over you, whose eyes move
only when I move?

3.

I wrap my arms around you, my cheek against your slashes,
and cower under a sudden storm.
I hold the strong, delicate sound of you

breathing in the lightning
and hard rain.

I have shrunk back
but you, while I held on,
have grown.

4.

Until I found you, I could not have told you
I would like to become an eye
in the white bark
where a limb fell.

5.

Until I found you, I thought you stood still.
But I have followed, and know
you drift and lean,
loving the wide grassy slopes
that smell mysteriously
of rain and elk
though neither are here.

- This poem is a bit unrealistically sappy

Time Zones

Evenings are large enough.
We cook, have dinner, and walk before losing the sun.
Tonight we took my favorite walk past the Finnish log
granaries that have weathered the century
sod chinked and upright beside the field road,
past the broken windmill at the homestead,
out to the ridge where we heard
two sandhill cranes whulping and crying below us,
settling into the grass for the night.
We're near a solstice, the generous one.
We followed the sun as it drifted upwind of us
like a slow oblivious bear, heading north
into Montana's Madison Range and vanishing
without a glance back.
We turned back when we could no longer see it
but I know it must be drifting
still in its sleepless haze toward the salmon
in Alaskan rivers where people will fish all night
without darkness.
Wearing your sunglasses at ten at night,
you spoke of the city: trillions of lights
flicked on and off, just like that, by people
who don't know their own hands.
I counted the lights in the north end of our valley —
all seven had come on.
As the night grew its enormous silence around us,
I thought of the splinter my hand absorbed
from an unoiled beam in the loft of Michaelangelo's
dark house in Cararra, where I once slept

near a man whose skin smelled of ocean and of olives,
whose hair was a thick black braid
and whose name was Dionysus.
A thought as placeless as migrating needlefish,
ephemeral as breath.

Mud Time

On the steep slippery bank between the river and the railroad tracks
where the train bums wander down looking for a place
to wash, make a small smouldering fire
to spread hands over and stare
into the flames until the absences of things become
the comfort of being nowhere,
I found a washing machine lying on its side like a fallen moon
half in the mud, half out. It was the old crank kind,
barrel round, it hummed in kitchens,
back porches, pre-spin cycle, the first white shine
of enamel now rain and rust stained like a tooth
darkened from rituals of smoke and drink.

I've seen washers like this on flatbeds at auctions,
the all-for-one-money heap auctioned at the end
when only the newlywed mennonites, the die-hard junk
junkies, and collectors of obsolete appliances
stick around to bid. And once I came by one peering
into the window of an abandoned farmhouse where daffodils
and grape hyacinths bloomed each spring
long after the hands that dug and packed the ground
around the bulbs dissolved to bone dust. All that season
I returned, welcome among those unseen women
who kept their home from crumbling:
the stern one turned the crank, wrung water from the blouses,
the tidy one took an apple bough, forked the wire line,

shook and hung the fleet of white
to flap dry in spring wind,
while the excitable one pressed her lips to the perennials,
asking about their winter.

The wringer was taken or missing in the mud of the washer
I found above the river, its lid long gone.
What lived inside —
beer and soup cans, cigarette butts, nests of slop,
spiders, wrappers, leaves.
Someone must have loved this machine once, the time,
the trips to the river it saved her.

Ohio Nocturne

in memory of James Wright

At the crossroads of the National Highway and Route 27
in southeastern Ohio,
it's almost midnight and a boy is mopping the floor of the cafe.
Although the sign on the door says OPEN,
everyone going elsewhere has gone,
asphalt and dust whispering under the wheels.
The boy is part of this loneliness.
He keeps a grass snake's grey skin
clasped to his beltloop like a string of keys. As slowly
as the minutes slink through town, he moves
the mop across the tiles, the scaly life left behind for another
swaying on his thigh. He doesn't notice me
looking into the cafe window
from the phone booth in the parking lot.
So he doesn't know how at home he looks
to someone on the other side: lost
in the legginess of adolescence,
the whole place to himself, the last wedge of pie
waiting in the refrigerated case,
the chairs legs up, twisted and stacked on tabletops—
their shadows spidering along the wall—
and the black and white floor tiles starting to glow,
ready for the quick slippered feet
of nervous girls.

Tonight, again, he practices all the angles
of a slow dance, learning to lead with his back
toward the place he's going.
He slips into the ache of rhythm, groin against her,
his palm tingling in the hollow of her arm.

He doesn't seem to mind how late it's gotten,
or the diesel odor of trucks, or the numb, continual whir
of the interstate several hills south.
He's in no real hurry,
under age in a dry county.
The mop swishes across the floor, following his lead,
erasing the footprints to himself.

It's May, and earlier today I saw the ferocious lavender
blossom of the redbud tree gathered along the highway.
Only May, and already this night is thick with crickets
singing in the sidewalk cracks, out-singing the dark
empty rattle of boxcars on the westbound track. One shiny
delirious beetle is thwacking the bulb of the booth
where I stand, even after the boy has flicked the cafe light,
locked up and gone.
One faithful green and black beetle
navigating the air between the receiver
and the silence on the other end.

Inland

Some mornings there's fog
folded over the slim boundaries of a clothesline in the yard.
It wanders through my sleeves and buttonholes,
it rubs the leaves, the gold stubbles of corn,
the weathered gate and beyond.
It is towing the ocean back to me,
inland, along rivers,
blue salt of loneliness and veins.

I see the fog slipping the ocean's small eggs
into the grass — each spire now glitters, now balances
a speck of the infinite —
and no odor of the sea is anywhere near.
And the animals drop their necks to graze,
a woman steps out to the mailbox, walks upon the fog,
crushes it, and I crush it going out to the road.
And the loneliness enters us too.
And the letter, the road, the glass of milk at breakfast
are also filled with it.

I watch the road
and wait for a shape to appear,
something to hold its own against the fog.
A school bus emerges, solid as the letter n
in a tonnage of vanishes,
the headlights searching for the asphalt.
Inside each face a blur.
The bus rumbles around the corner, passes me,

I wave and the leaves shudder away in the wake.
What is loneliness
but the loss of visibility?

                                        Through a small window I listen
to the men shoveling coal into the cellars of sleep.
The hollow sound I awaken to.
The bones in their fingers ache,
their breath slips away, gray ribbons
from their lungs braiding into the fog.
We share a cigarette on the stoop
but we don't smoke the loneliness out of us,
we don't burn it away with tobacco, speech, coal.

Mangoes

I learned to eat mangoes from my mother.
I learned to eat them from a small plate
under the bedside light when it was late and the moon
and I were sleepless.
I watched her suck and slurp the mango's beauty,
as if she were eating the moon or her own children.
She carved and devoured
the agreeable pulp and I feared her
hunger, the imprint of teeth in skin.
I eat mangos for the sound through my lips is a lullaby,
the sweet juice is an ointment, a slick thread
I lick and erase
between her chin and mine.

I pull at the mango's radiant meat as if it were a sunset,
gnawing my way in to the armor, the darker pit.
I am unlearning the fear
she taught me about being born.
If I were my mother I would toss this pit
to the mulch heap in the morning,
let it soften and split apart
to free the innermost, imprisoned seed.

But I swallow the small seed and dream my mother walks
hand in hand with a child who leads her.
Her thick ankles are turning slender
as a young woman's again.
The sand and rock rub back
the dead under her feet,
and I see that her shine and her oldness are coming at once,

the way a banister is rubbed smooth
from hundreds of hands, or from the same hand
hundreds of times. I see that my power is not a gift
but something I have died for in the fertile dark
and will again, leaving her behind.

Full Circle

Naked, I am waiting for the moon beyond the window,
waiting for the slow hollow glow to rise, whole, and fill the sky.
I, too, took a long time to be born,
and my mother, weakened with the pain of me,
kept rising and falling, her breath and her wide muscles whistling
like a dark wind across the sage.
She pushed until I was a pair of lips and a cry.
She slipped back weeping, and I broke
from the rock of her thighs.

Tonight I have grown into a slender window
of bones, my flesh gathered from dust, snow
that carves the mountain. I have eyes
the moon begins to open all through my body.
I am giving birth to my mother, a child
the stars curl into when the moon
roams and presses its light against me.
She is the first larkspur, the yellow violet pushing
tentative into the air,
hearty and delicate offspring of soil.
She is the voice floating under the wing of the nighthawk.

My power comes from opening my thighs,
letting the moon migrate through my body, seed my blood,
letting the wind harden and fill my breasts with nursing voices.
I will not be the same once the moon has risen
and drifted through me, once the elk have wandered
through my hair as I am sleeping,
matting the grass with their tongues,
rubbing their antlers down into my eyelashes.
Nor will I be the same once I have watched my mother die.
She is a blue fold and recedes like old snow,

she is losing her last child,
her own mother, whom she has carried
for half a century, stubbornly,
unborn in herself.

Daughter

I hear her
splintering like the seed inside
the pinecone, the furious grease
inside the smoke and speed of the fire
of our bodies. The hard red seed of her,
her pink nipple, her penis-husk,
her odors and hairs,
her molecular dust,
her dream file, her first and last word,
her undiscussed deja vus,
her lovers and scorners,
the ones her unformed fingers navigate or swiftly shun,
her gravity gathered from the moon
shivering across our backs and buttocks:
whoever she is
I hear her
in a moment's galactic after-stretch,
in the flatness of exile when your body recedes
like the mollusk oozing back
into its own space upon touch.
She is imprinted with our silence,
the scent of our tongues,
she comes home to our breath's cradle,
sifts through our pores
bringing only her memory
which she will lose
as she grows into my body,
bringing only the smoke of her name.
Having come from the sperm of you,
not you,
and from the black infinite ash of my egg,
she is more egg than sperm,

more than lips or the sound sex makes,
though it will be a long time before she whispers
her name through my skin.
I listen longer than you,
long after you and she are sleeping,
I listen to my fear,
and smell it,
and it is the forest
I was born in
burning like an eyelash.

Between Towns is the winner of the 1991 first-book competition in the TTUP Poetry Award Series. The competition was supported generously by The CH Foundation and the Helen Jones Foundation in honor of the sisters Christine DeVitt and Helen DeVitt Jones.